5-03   6x(

S0-CCJ-113

# The Galapagos Islands

Greg Roza

SAN DIEGO PUBLIC LIBRARY

3 1336 06174 1535

The Rosen Publishing Group's

**READING ROOM**
*Collection*™

New York

Published in 2003 by The Rosen Publishing Group, Inc.
29 East 21st Street, New York, NY 10010

Copyright © 2003 by The Rosen Publishing Group, Inc.

First Library Edition 2003

All rights reserved. No part of this book may be reproduced in any form without permission in writing from the publisher, except by a reviewer.

Book Design: Haley Wilson

Photo Credits: Cover, pp. 1, 2–3, 22–23, 24 © Galen Rowell/Corbis; pp. 4–5 © PictureQuest; p. 6 © James Davis/Corbis; pp. 8–9 © Tui DeRoy/Bruce Coleman, Inc./PictureQuest; p. 11 © Mark Newman/International Stock; pp. 12–13 © The Image Bank; p. 14 © Christine Osborne/Corbis; p. 15 © Wolfgang Kaehler/Corbis; p. 16 © Dave Wade/FPG International; pp. 18–19 © Bettmann/ Corbis; pp. 20–21 © Kevin Schafer/Corbis; p. 20 (top and middle insets) © Frank Lane Picture Agency/Corbis; p. 20 (bottom inset) © Galen Rowell/Corbis; p. 21 (Charles Darwin) © Michael Nicholson/Corbis.

Library of Congress Cataloging-in-Publication Data

Roza, Greg
   The Galapagos islands / Greg Roza.
       p.  cm. — (The Rosen Publishing Group's reading room collection)
Includes index.
Summary:  This book describes the Galapagos Islands, telling of the islands' formation, the plants and animals that are on the islands, and the findings of Charles Darwin as he studied the wildlife of the islands.
   ISBN 0-8239-3714-3
   1.  Natural history—Galapagos Islands—Juvenile
literature    2.  Galapagos Islands—Juvenile literature
[1.  Natural history—Galapagos Islands    2.  Galapagos Islands]
I. Title   II. Series
   QH198.G3.R69  2003                              2001-007682
   508.866—dc21

Manufactured in the United States of America

**For More Information**
Galapagos Islands (The Charles Darwin Foundation): Kid's Corner
http://www.darwinfoundation.org/misc/kids/kids.html

Galapagos Islands Wildlife Refuge
http://www.spacelab.net/~cni/indexnav.html

# Contents

# A Very Special Place

The Galapagos (guh-LAH-puh-gohs) Islands are a part of Ecuador (EHK-wuh-door), a country in South America. The islands are located on the **equator** about 600 miles west of Ecuador, in the Pacific Ocean. There are five large islands, eight medium-sized islands, six small islands, and many more very small islands. Altogether, the Galapagos Islands have a total land area of about 3,000 square miles.

The five main Galapagos Islands—from the largest to the smallest—are Isabela, Santa Cruz, Fernandina, Santiago, and San Cristobal.

There is no other place like the Galapagos Islands. Scientists and sightseers have visited the islands since they were discovered in 1535. Visitors come to the islands to see colorful animals, ancient land formations, and beautiful scenery. Scientists come to the Galapagos Islands to study a place that is unlike any other on Earth.

The Galapagos Islands

Santiago

Fernandina

Santa Cruz

Isabela

San Cristobal

## Shield Volcano

layers
of
rock

water level

magma

Many of the Galapagos Islands are shield volcanoes.
A shield volcano is wide and not very steep, and looks
like an upside-down bowl.

# How Were the Islands Formed?

The Galapagos Islands are actually **volcanoes**! Islands like the Galapagos form when liquid rock called **magma** flows out of a crack in Earth's **crust** at the bottom of the ocean. Scientists call these cracks in Earth's crust "hot spots."

The magma is called **lava** once it comes out of Earth's crust. The lava cools and forms a layer of solid rock. The layers of hardened lava build higher and higher on top of each other over the hot spot. After many years, the layers of rock rise above the surface of the ocean, forming new land masses. These land masses are volcanic islands.

When volcanic islands are new, their land is very rocky. It is hard for plants and animals to live there. Over many years, the volcanic rock breaks down to form soil. Then plants can start to grow. Birds and other animals are then able to **survive** on the islands by eating the plants.

Beneath the Galapagos Islands, Earth's crust is moving to the west very slowly all the time. Earth's crust actually floats on a layer of magma. Because of this, the hot spot below the Galapagos Islands moves west along with Earth's crust. This is how the hot spot has formed a chain, or line, of volcanic islands.

Because of **erosion**, the Galapagos Islands will one day sink back into the ocean as newer islands rise up. This takes many, many years. In fact, there were once more islands than there are now. Some of the islands sank into the ocean about 9 million years ago and are now more than a mile underwater.

Some of the Galapagos Islands still have active volcanoes on them. An eruption occurred on Isabela Island in October 1998.

Scientists believe that the Galapagos Islands are between 3.5 and 5 million years old. This may seem very old, but it is actually young for volcanic islands. The eastern islands are the oldest islands. Fernandina is the youngest of the islands and may only be about 700,000 years old.

# Life on the Galapagos Islands

Since the Galapagos Islands were discovered, few people have lived there. Over the years, the islands have been used as a rest stop for explorers, **pirates**, and whale and seal hunters. Scientists have always been interested in the special features of the islands. However, the living conditions on the Galapagos Islands are hard, and not many people have stayed there for long.

Ecuador officially claimed the islands in 1832. A few small colonies soon formed. Today, about 15,000 people live on the Galapagos Islands. Most of these people live on the island of Santa Cruz. In 1995, the government of Ecuador limited the number of visitors who could come to the islands each year to 60,000 people. They did this to protect the islands from harm.

The sea is important to people on the Galapagos Islands. Some people make their living by fishing. The people depend on the sea for much of the food they eat.

The Galapagos Islands are best known for their colorful and unusual wildlife. The wildlife on the Galapagos Islands is special because it changed gradually over millions of years, separated from the rest of the world. Some of the plants and animals found on the islands cannot be found anywhere else on Earth. In fact, the wildlife is often different from island to island.

Spanish explorers named the Galapagos Islands after the giant tortoises they found when they arrived there. "*Galapagos*" is Spanish for "tortoise."

Perhaps the most well-known animal on the Galapagos Islands is the giant **tortoise** (TOHR-tuss). A giant tortoise can be up to six feet long, can weigh over 500 pounds, and can live for more than 200 years! They are able to live up to a year without food and water. The Spanish explorers who first visited the islands found about 250,000 tortoises living on the rocky land. These explorers loaded their ships with giant tortoises to use for food on long sea journeys.

Hundreds of thousands of **iguanas** live on the Galapagos Islands. Many scientists believe that iguanas were probably the first type of animal to live there. The Galapagos Islands are home to the **marine** iguana, the only iguana in the world that lives in water for part of its life. Marine iguanas usually stay close to shore, but some male iguanas have been known to dive as deep as forty feet and stay underwater for up to thirty minutes!

The islands are home to a large number of birds, including finches, hawks, and herons. Visitors to the Galapagos Islands may also get to see the only type of penguin that lives on the equator.

**Prickly Pear Cactus**

Other animals living on or around the Galapagos Islands include many kinds of shellfish, sharks, dolphins, whales, snakes, and giant grasshoppers.

# Land Iguana

The Galapagos Islands are also home to many different kinds of plants. The prickly pear is a cactus that grows on lava rocks and is eaten by the giant tortoise and the land iguana.

# How the Plants and Animals Got There

The Galapagos Islands were never connected to the continent of South America. Because of this, people have often wondered how all the plants and animals got there in the first place.

Animals that live in the waters around the islands—like seals, tortoises, and penguins—were probably carried there from South America on fast sea currents. Bugs, spiders, birds, and bats might have been blown out to the islands by strong winds during storms. Sea birds could have flown that far by themselves. Land animals like iguanas, rats, and some bugs may have floated across the sea on large pieces of land that broke off from South America.

Seeds may have been carried to the Galapagos Islands in different ways. Birds probably brought many seeds with them, or strong winds could have blown seeds across the sea from South America.

Darwin wasn't paid for his work on this trip, and he was seasick for most of the journey! However, the things he discovered on the Galapagos Islands helped to make him one of the most famous scientists in history.

18

# Darwin and the *Beagle*

No one had studied the Galapagos Islands and their wildlife until 1835. That year, a young scientist named Charles Darwin arrived at the islands on a ship called the *Beagle.* The captain of the *Beagle* was sailing around South America so he could study and map that area of the world. The Galapagos Islands were just one stop on a four-year trip.

Darwin joined the crew of the *Beagle* to collect information about the plants, animals, and **fossils** on the coasts of South America. The *Beagle* landed at the Galapagos Islands to gather tortoises for fresh food on the trip home. Darwin and the rest

Charles Darwin

of the crew stayed on the islands for five weeks. During this time, Darwin studied the wildlife on four of the islands and made many important discoveries.

In 1859, Darwin published his discoveries and ideas. His findings changed the way most scientists looked at the world.

During his brief stay on the Galapagos Islands, Darwin saw animals he had never seen anywhere else in the world. He was even more surprised by the differences he found in animals from one island to the next.

Among the wildlife he studied, Darwin noticed thirteen types of finches. A finch is a small bird. The finches all looked the same except for small differences in the size and shape of their beaks. This led Darwin to believe that the finches all originally came from a single kind of finch that had come to the islands millions of years earlier. Darwin believed that as time passed, the finches— as well as the other animals on the islands— **developed** the features that best helped them to survive. The animals with features that did not help them survive died off over time, leaving the stronger animals to pass their features on to their young.

Charles Darwin

# The Future of the Galapagos Islands

Even though it has remained the same for millions of years, life on the Galapagos Islands is beginning to change as more and more people come to the islands. When Spanish explorers first arrived on the islands, about 250,000 tortoises lived there. Now there are fewer than 15,000. Hunters and fishermen have destroyed many animals for their own benefit. Curious visitors and growing communities on the islands continue to place the wildlife in danger. New animals that have been brought to the islands—especially goats, rats, and dogs—have killed many of the local animals.

In 1959, the Galapagos Islands became a national park and a wildlife reserve. Even though the human population of the islands continues to increase every year, many concerned scientists want to protect the Galapagos Islands and their rare wildlife for future generations to study and enjoy.

# Glossary

**crust**    The top layer of Earth.

**develop**    To change and grow gradually.

**equator**    An imaginary line around the middle of Earth that separates it into two parts, north and south. Areas on or near the equator are always hot.

**erosion**    The process of being worn away a little at a time by water and wind.

**fossil**    The hardened remains of a dead animal or plant that lived long ago.

**iguana**    A kind of large lizard.

**lava**    Hot liquid rock that comes out of a volcano.

**magma**    Hot liquid rock beneath Earth's surface.

**marine**    Having to do with the sea.

**pirate**    Someone who attacks and robs ships.

**survive**    To continue to exist.

**tortoise**    A turtle that lives on land.

**volcano**    An opening in Earth's crust through which melted rock is sometimes forced.

# Index

## A
animal(s), 5, 7, 12, 13, 14, 17, 19, 21, 22

## B
*Beagle*, 19
bird(s), 7, 14, 17, 21

## D
Darwin, Charles, 19, 21

## E
Ecuador, 4, 10
equator, 4, 14
erosion, 8
explorers, 10, 13, 22

## F
Fernandina, 9
finch(es), 14, 21

## I
iguana(s), 14, 17

## L
lava, 7

## M
magma, 7, 8

## N
national park, 22

## P
Pacific Ocean, 4
penguin(s), 14, 17
pirates, 10

## S
Santa Cruz, 10
scientists, 5, 7, 9, 10, 14, 22
South America, 4, 17, 19
Spanish, 13, 22

## T
tortoise(s), 13, 17, 19, 22

## V
volcanic islands, 7, 8, 9
volcanoes, 7

## W
wildlife, 12, 19, 21, 22